Book brief

1 Set in New England in the early 1860s, this novel by American writer Louisa May Alcott was an immediate success.

2 The story follows the lives of Mrs. March and her four daughters while Mr. March, their father, is away in the American Civil War.

3 The story presents a different idea of women compared to the traditional role of women in the 19th century.

4 Mrs. March encourages her daughters to work and to have happy lives whether they're married or not.

5 Main themes include growing up and the importance of family.

www.eligradedreaders.com

In this reader:

 **21st Century Skills** — To encourage students to connect the story to the world they live in.

Preliminary — B1 level activities.

Story Notes — A brief summary of the text.

Glossary — Explanation of difficult words.

Picture Caption — A brief explanation of the picture.

Audio — These icons indicate the parts of the story that are recorded. start ■ stop

Think — To encourage students to develop their critical thinking skills.

The FSC® certification guarantees that the paper used in these publications comes from certified forests, promoting responsible forestry management worldwide.

MIX
Paper from responsible sources
FSC® C127663

For this series of ELI graded readers, we have planted 5000 new trees.

Louisa May Alcott

Little Women

Retold and Activities by
Silvana Sardi

Illustrated by
Júlia Sardà

Teen ELi Readers

Teen Eli Readers

The **ELI Readers** collection is a complete range of books and plays for readers of all ages, ranging from captivating contemporary stories to timeless classics. There are four series, each catering for a different age group: **First ELI Readers, Young ELI Readers, Teen ELI Readers** and **Young Adult ELI Readers**. The books are carefully edited and beautifully illustrated to capture the essence of the stories and plots. The readers are supplemented with 'Focus on' texts packed with background cultural information about the writers and their lives and times.

Little Women
by **Louisa May Alcott**
Illustrated by **Júlia Sardà**
Language Level Consultant by
Alison Smith
Retold and Activities by
Silvana Sardi

ELI Readers
Founder and Series Editors
Paola Accattoli, Grazia Ancillani, Daniele Garbuglia (Art Director)

Graphic Design
**Andersen
the Premedia Company**

Production Manager
Francesco Capitano

Photo credits
Shutterstock

New edition: **2021**
First edition: **2015**

© ELI s.r.l.
P.O. Box 6
62019 Recanati MC
Italy
T +39 071750701
F +39 071977851
info@elionline.com
www.elionline.com

Typeset in 12 / 17 pt
Fulmar designed by Leo Philp

Printed in Italy by
**Tecnostampa - Pigini Group
Printing Division
Loreto - Trevi
ERT327.10
ISBN 978-88-536-3218-0**

Contents

6	**Main Characters**	
8	**Before you read**	
10	**Chapter 1**	*Christmas Time*
18	**Activities**	
20	**Chapter 2**	*Good Neighbors*
28	**Activities**	
30	**Chapter 3**	*Lazy Days*
38	**Activities**	
40	**Chapter 4**	*Busy Bees*
48	**Activities**	
50	**Chapter 5**	*Dark Days*
58	**Activities**	
60	**Chapter 6**	*Peaceful Weeks*
70	**Activities**	
72	**Focus on…**	*Louisa May Alcott*
74	**Focus on…**	*CLIL History* *The American Civil War*
76	**Focus on…**	*Little Women* *Success over the Years*
78	**Test Yourself**	
79	**Syllabus**	

Main Characters

Mrs. Margaret March
A kind woman who teaches her daughters that love and respect are the most important things in life.

Meg
A pretty girl, Meg, is the eldest of the sisters and likes nice things.

Jo
Very direct and a bit wild, Jo loves reading and writing stories.

Amy
The youngest of the sisters, Amy is a bit selfish and loves drawing.

Beth
A sweet, shy girl, Beth loves playing the piano.

Reading B1 Preliminary

1 Read about *Little Women*. Choose the best answer, A, B, C or D to complete the text.

Little Women is a book about family ____life____ . The story is about four sisters **(1)** _____ grow up in a poor family and are always trying to find ways to **(2)** _____ some money.
Their father is away at war, so the four girls try and help their mother as **(3)** _____ as they can. The girls have all got very different characters. Meg, the **(4)** _____ , is sixteen years old and is very pretty. She helps the family **(5)** _____ teaching children. Jo, on the other hand, is tall and slim and often acts more like a boy. She looks **(6)** _____ an old lady but doesn't find it very interesting. Beth, thirteen years old, is the quietest of them **(7)** _____ . She's shy and peaceful and most of the **(8)** _____ lives in a world of her own. Amy, the youngest, is also the **(9)** _____ beautiful and she knows it! With her blue eyes and long, blonde, curly hair, she feels very important and always acts like a young lady. **(10)** _____ all these differences and all their problems, Mrs. March manages to keep the family together.

	A	B	C	D
	A parents	B life	C relationship	D house
1	A which	B whose	C who	D where
2	A earn	B do	C arrange	D involve
3	A many	B lots	C few	D much
4	A most old	B elder	C older	D eldest
5	A with	B by	C at	D for
6	A for	B at	C to	D after
7	A all	B every	C each	D both
8	A days	B hours	C time	D period
9	A such	B much	C most	D very
10	A Unless	B Anyway	C But	D Despite

8

Writing

2 ***Little Women*** **is about the life of the March family. Read these questions and write your answers.**

1 Describe the place where you live. Do you like it? Why? / Why not?
2 Who do you live with and what do you do with your family in your free time?
3 Who has the same kind of character as you?
4 How much time do you spend with your family and how much with your friends?
5 What kind of things do you have to do at home to help with the housework?
6 Would you like to live on your own? Why? / Why not?

21st Century Skills

Listening

▶ 2 **3 Listen to the start of Chapter 1 and decide if these sentences are true (T) or false (F).**

		T	F
	The girls are talking about Christmas.	☑	☐
1	Meg would like to be rich.	☐	☐
2	The girls will receive lots of presents at Christmas.	☐	☐
3	Their mother is with their father.	☐	☐
4	Jo likes reading.	☐	☐
5	Amy is the artist of the family.	☐	☐
6	Their father has always been poor.	☐	☐

Chapter 1

Christmas Time

▶ 2 "I hate being poor when it's Christmas," complained Meg, looking down at her old dress.

"I know; Christmas without presents just won't be the same," said Jo.

The four sisters are talking about the poor Christmas they're going to have this year. Their father is away at war and they only have a dollar each to buy something for themselves.

"It's not fair that other girls have lots of nice things," said Amy sadly.

"But we've got Father and Mother and each other," said Beth quietly from her corner.

All four girls were sitting around the fire in the living room. They were waiting for their mother to come home. Their father was away at war like many others.

"Father won't be with us," said Meg. "Marmee[1] says that this is going to be a hard winter for everybody, especially for all the soldiers in the army. That's why we must forget about presents."

For a moment, they all thought about what they wanted for Christmas. They each had a dollar. Jo wanted a new book; Meg, something pretty to wear; Beth, some new music for her piano; Amy, some new pencils to draw with.

▶ **Beth, Jo, Amy and Meg are sitting around the fire talking about how sad Christmas is going to be without presents. They're knitting socks for the army.**

[1] **Marmee** mother (in this story)

Louisa May Alcott

Their father had been a rich man once, but had lost all his money when the girls were still little.

▶ 3

Their father had lost all his money a long time ago and now they're poor. When they see how old their mother's slippers are they each decide to buy her a present instead of something for themselves.

"I'd love to go and fight with Papa[1], instead of staying here and knitting socks for the army," said Jo.

"Oh, Jo!" said Beth, laughing. "You're more like a brother than a sister to us, so we need you here to protect us."

They all laughed, then suddenly, Amy looked at the clock on the wall above the fire and saw that it was 6 o'clock. The girls immediately forgot all their worries and Beth put her mother's slippers[2] near the fire. "Marmee really needs new slippers; these ones are so old," she said.

"I'll buy her new slippers for Christmas," said Jo immediately.

"No, I will, I'm the eldest," said Meg.

"Why don't we all buy her something instead of a present for ourselves?" suggested Beth.

"What a wonderful idea, Beth!" said the others all together.

"I'll buy her some gloves," said Meg.

"I'll get her new slippers," said Jo.

"I want to give her some handkerchiefs," said Beth.

[1] **Papa** Father
[2] **slippers**

Little Women

"And I'll give her a little bottle of perfume[1] so I'll have some money left to buy my pencils," said Amy.

The others all laughed. Amy was the youngest so she was allowed to be a little selfish.

It would be a lovely surprise for their mother. They decided to go shopping the following afternoon. Then the girls started talking about the play they were preparing for Christmas night. It was a family tradition and they always all had fun. When Mrs. March arrived that evening, she found her four lovely daughters chatting happily around the fire.

That night she had a special surprise for them: a letter from their father. It was full of stories about camp life, but he never complained once about anything. Everyone cried at the end and missed him even more.

"I'll try and not be wild, and be what he loves to call me, 'a little woman', and do my duty here," said Jo.

Before going to bed, Beth played the old piano and they all sang as they did every night.

Christmas morning arrived and Jo woke up first.

The girls always put on a play on Christmas night. When Mrs. March gets home she reads a letter to them from their father. They all miss him. Jo says she'll try to be 'a little woman' which is what her father always calls her, instead of being wild.

[1] perfume

Louisa May Alcott

She called the others and they went downstairs to see their mother, but she wasn't there.

"She's probably out helping someone," said Hannah, who had lived with them since Meg was born, and was more of a friend than a servant[1] to them all. Just then, Mrs. March came in.

"Merry Christmas, my lovely girls," she said, kissing each of them.

"Where have you been?" asked Jo.

"Near here, there's a mother with six hungry children, and a baby. They have nothing to eat or drink. Will you give them your breakfast, my sweet daughters, as a Christmas present?" asked Mrs. March. She already knew they'd say yes and soon they were all carrying baskets of food over to the unfortunate family. When they arrived at the Hummel's poor house, Hannah made a fire and the girls gave the hungry children the food. Once back home, the girls had bread and milk for their Christmas breakfast, but they were happy, especially when they gave their mother the presents they had bought.

That evening the girls had fun acting for their friends. At the end of the play, Mrs. March told

On Christmas morning, the girls and their mother take their breakfast to a poor family who have nothing. Back at home the girls only have bread and milk for their Christmas breakfast but they're happy especially when they give their mother her presents from them.

Mrs. March, Hannah and the four girls are going to the poor family's house with food and wood to make a fire.

---

[1] **servant** a person paid to help with the cleaning and cooking

Louisa May Alcott

Their neighbor[1], Mr Laurence sends them nice things to eat as they were so kind to the poor family. They don't know him or his grandson very well.

them all to come to the kitchen for supper.

Everybody was surprised to see the table full of ice cream, cakes, biscuits, sweets and chocolates. "When old Mr. Laurence heard what you did for the Hummels, he decided to send you these things," explained their mother.

Mr. Laurence was an old gentleman who lived in the big house next door with his grandson, but they didn't know them very well.

"Remember when the cat ran away and the grandson brought it back?" asked Jo. "We started talking, then he saw Meg coming and walked off. We must try and speak to him, I'm sure he's lonely," she said.

Meg and Jo are invited to a party. They're pretty even if their clothes are old. Jo doesn't really care what she looks like. Meg wears shoes with high heels even if they hurt her.

Next morning, Meg and Jo received an invitation to a party on New Year's Eve. Meg was very excited but also worried about Jo's dress. Like hers, it was old, but at least Meg's wasn't burnt at the back. Jo, who didn't care so much, promised to stand against the wall all night. The night of the party, the girls looked very pretty despite their unfashionable clothes. Meg put on high-heeled shoes which hurt her, but she wore them just the same.

---

[1] **neighbor (US)** the person who lives in the house next to yours
   neighbour (UK)

Little Women

At the party Meg talked to the other girls. Jo stood against the wall. She was bored so found a dark corner to hide in. Suddenly, she realized there was somebody else there. It was the "Laurence boy"! They both laughed and soon they were having fun talking about everybody at the party. Laurie seemed interested in Meg and said how pretty she was. Then, Jo heard Meg calling her. She was sitting on a sofa, holding her ankle. She couldn't walk.

"I knew you'd hurt yourself with those shoes. Now, how am I going to get you home?" said Jo.

"Don't worry," said Laurie, "I'll take you home in my grandfather's carriage[1]."

"Oh no, it's so early! You can't want to leave the party already," said Meg.

"Don't worry, I always go home early," said Laurie.

So that night, the girls went home in a beautiful carriage; the perfect end to a brilliant evening.

However, next day, both girls had to go back to work; Meg to the four spoilt children she taught, and Jo to Aunt March, who was always in a bad mood.

At the party Jo meets Laurie, their neighbor and they start chatting. He seems interested in Meg. Then Meg hurts her ankle and Laurie takes them home in his grandfather's carriage. The next day the two girls have to go back to work.

Think
Do you like going to parties? Why / Why not?

[1] carriage

After-reading Activities • Chapter 1

Reading Comprehension

1 Match the sentences with the person who said them. Then, put them in order (1 to 7) as they happen in Chapter 1.

1. [A] Merry Christmas, my lovely girls.
2. [ ] I'll buy her some gloves.
3. [ ] Don't worry, I always go home early.
4. [ ] She's probably out helping someone.
5. [ ] Why don't we all buy her something instead of a present for ourselves?
6. [ ] I'd love to go and fight with Papa, instead of staying here and knitting socks for the army.
7. [ ] And I'll give her a little bottle of perfume so I'll have some money left to buy my pencils.

A Marmee
B Amy
C Beth
D Jo
E Meg
F Laurie
G Hannah

Reading B1 Preliminary

2 Complete the text about Chapter 1 with one word in each space.

Mrs. March was very kind and she had _taught_ her daughters to be the same. Therefore, on Christmas morning the girls (**1**) _____ happy to give their breakfast to a poor family. Then, their neighbor, Mr. Laurence, sent lots of nice things (**2**) _____ them to eat on Christmas evening after hearing (**3**) _____ kind they had been. On New Year's Eve, Meg and Jo went (**4**) _____ a party. They met Mr. Laurence's grandson there, (**5**) _____ took them home in (**6**) _____ grandfather's carriage after Meg hurt her ankle.

Writing

21st Century Skills

3 A **Write four short descriptions of the sisters, Meg, Jo, Beth and Amy. Talk about:**

- their character
- their hobbies and interests

3 B **Now say which sister you prefer and why.**

_____
_____
_____
_____
_____
_____

Before-reading Activity

Vocabulary

4 Read the sentences and complete the words which all appear in Chapter 2.

	A place with plants and flowers.	<u>g a r d e n</u>
1	Something sweet to eat, usually made with flour.	c _ _ _
2	A person you don't know.	s _ _ _ _ _ _ _
3	The person who lives in the house next to yours.	n _ _ _ _ _ _ _
4	A talking bird.	p _ _ _ _ _
5	A place full of books.	l _ _ _ _ _ _
6	A short written message.	n _ _ _

Chapter 2

Good Neighbors

Jo sees Laurie at the window. He seems sad so she throws a snowball at the window, which makes him smile. He asks Jo to come and visit since he's been ill and her mother lets her go.

▶ 4 One snowy day, Jo went out to the garden to clean the path. The Marches' old, brown house was next to Mr. Laurence's, with a low wall separating the two gardens. Jo often thought that the Laurence house was tidier and more beautiful than theirs, but too quiet. She hadn't seen Laurie since the party and wondered if he ever felt lonely in that big house. Then, looking up, she saw him at the upstairs window. He seemed sad so she made a little snowball, and threw it at Laurie's window. The boy smiled and opened the window.

"Hey, are you sick?" shouted Jo.

"I'm better now, thank you. I've had a bad cold and haven't been out for a week."

"I'm sorry. What do you do all day?"

"Nothing, I'm so bored."

"Does nobody come and visit you?"

"No. Will you come?"

"If Mother will let me. I'll go and ask her. Close the window and wait for me. I'll be back soon."

Jo ran to look for her mother, who happily said

Little Women

yes. A minute later, Jo was in Laurie's room with a cake from Meg and Beth's kittens to play with.

"I often see you all sitting around the fire in the evening with your mother," said Laurie. "She seems so sweet." He was silent for a moment then said, "You know, I haven't got a mother."

Jo felt sorry for him and said, "Instead of looking at us through the window, you must come and visit. Everybody would love to meet you! Wouldn't your grandpa let you?"

"I think so. It's just that he doesn't want me to bother strangers," said Laurie.

"We aren't strangers, we're your neighbors, and you wouldn't bother us at all," said Jo.

"Grandpa isn't bad; he just lives among his books. Then, there's Mr. Brooke, my teacher, but he doesn't stay here, so I'm usually at home on my own."

"Well, that's no good, you ought to go out more. Forget about being shy," said Jo in her usual direct way. Laurie smiled, happy to have this new friend. Jo told him about Aunt March, with her talking parrot and spoilt dog. She also discovered that Laurie loved books like her.

Laurie often watches the March family sitting together around the fire. He doesn't have a mother and feels lonely because his grandpa reads all the time and the only other person who comes to the house is his teacher, Mr. Brooke. Jo says he must come to their house.

Louisa May Alcott

While Jo is in the library, Mr. Laurence comes in. She thinks it's Laurie and says she isn't afraid of his grandpa. The old man laughs and says she's like her grandfather. Mr. Laurence then visits Mrs. March and they become good neighbors.

"Come and see our library," said Laurie. "You needn't be afraid, Grandpa is out."

"I'm not afraid of anything," said Jo, laughing.

The library was a lovely room full of books, pictures and statues. Laurie left Jo alone there for a moment to speak to his doctor. While she was looking at a big picture of Laurie's grandpa on the wall, she heard the door opening behind her. Without turning, she said, "I'm sure I shouldn't be afraid of your grandpa, he's got kind eyes."

"Thank you, madam," said a man's voice. It was Laurie's grandfather! Jo turned, her face red. For once, she didn't know what to say.

"So, you're not afraid of me, hey?"

"Not much, sir."

"So, you like me!" said the old man laughing. Jo relaxed and began to chat happily.

"You're like your grandfather, young girl. He was a kind, honest man. Tell your mother I'll come and see her one day," said Mr. Laurence.

Jo certainly would, and she couldn't wait to tell her sisters all about her special day at the Laurence's.

A few days later, Mr. Laurence came to see Mrs. March and they became good neighbors. He said

Little Women

that her girls could come and visit any time as he was happy Laurie had such good friends.

Meg loved walking in his garden; Jo loved his library; Amy tried to copy his pictures; only Beth was too shy to go to the house. Then, one day, Mr. Laurence came and asked Beth if she would come and play his piano sometimes, as Laurie didn't want to play anymore.

Beth was so excited that she forgot to be shy, and putting her small hand in his, walked to his house.

"I had a little girl once, with eyes like yours," said Mr. Laurence, as he led Beth to the piano.

After that, Beth went to play every day and forgot to be afraid. Weeks later, she decided to make slippers for the old man to thank him. When they were finished, she left them in his study with a short, simple note. Two days later, a piano arrived for Beth with this letter:

"Dear Madam,
My slippers are beautiful. This piano once belonged to the little granddaughter I lost. I want you to have it now. Your friend,
James Laurence."

> Mr. Laurence tells the girls they can come to his house whenever they want. At first Beth is too shy to go, then Mr. Laurence asks her to come and play his piano and she goes. Beth makes slippers for the old man and he gives her a piano which belonged to his little granddaughter who died.

Louisa May Alcott

Beth forgets about being shy and thanks the old man by kissing him on the cheek. Mr. Laurence feels as if he's found his granddaughter again.

To everyone's surprise, shy, little Beth went straight to Mr. Laurence in his study. Remembering the little girl he had lost, she put her arms around his neck and kissed him on the cheek. The old man was so pleased that he sat her on his knee, and feeling as if he had found his granddaughter again, they talked together until it was time for her to go home.

While Beth had made a new friend, Amy wasn't happy at all. First, her teacher had been angry with her for eating sweets in class. Then, one Saturday afternoon, Amy saw Meg and Jo getting ready to go out.

"Where are you going?" she asked.

"Little girls shouldn't ask questions," answered Jo.

"Oh, Meg, please tell me! I'm bored and want to come too," said Amy.

"I'm sorry Amy. I can't tell you. It's a secret," said Meg kindly.

Laurie had invited the girls to the theater[1] and Jo wanted to have fun, not look after Amy.

"Look, Amy," said Jo angrily, "you're too young to come with us."

Amy isn't happy like Beth. She got into trouble at school for eating sweets in class and now Meg and Jo are going out and they won't even tell her where they're going. Jo wants to have fun at the theater, not look after Amy and she shouts at her little sister.

Beth comes to say thank you to Mr. Laurence for the piano he sent her. He holds her in his arms like he used to do with his little granddaughter he once had.

[1] **theater (US) theatre (UK)** a building or outdoor area in which plays and other performances are given

24

Louisa May Alcott

Then Laurie arrived and as the two girls left, Amy shouted:

"You'll be sorry for this, Jo!"

Jo didn't realize[1] how serious her sister was, until the next day.

Jo sat down at her desk to write another story in her little book, but couldn't find it. She had written three short stories so far and wanted to finish the book for her father's return. She looked in the drawer – nothing. Then she remembered Amy's words. She ran downstairs shouting:

"Amy, where's my book?"

"I don't know and I don't care!" said Amy.

"Don't tell lies, Amy. What have you done with it?"

"I burnt it in the fire last night," said Amy.

Jo had never felt so angry. She shook Amy hard, saying:

"I'll never forgive you for this!"

Meg ran to help Amy, while Beth went to Jo. That evening, Amy tried to say she was sorry, but Jo refused to speak to her. Jo was so like her mother.

Mrs. March used to get angry a lot when she was a girl, but over the years she had learned to

Amy is so angry with Jo that she burns the book of stories Jo was writing for her father. Then she tries to say she's sorry, but Jo refuses to speak to her.

[1] **realize (US)** understand
realise (UK)

Little Women

control herself, and now, instead of shouting, she kept her lips shut tight.

Next day, Jo decided to go skating[1] on the frozen river with Laurie. Amy followed her because she still wanted Jo to forgive her. At the river, Jo saw Amy coming, but she didn't wait for her. Laurie was in front and said:

"Don't go skating in the middle, the ice is too thin."

Jo heard him, but Amy didn't. She was still too far away. Then, there was a terrible scream. Jo turned and saw Amy in the middle of the river. The ice was breaking and Amy was disappearing into the water below. Jo was so frightened, she couldn't move. Luckily, Laurie was there. He pulled Amy out of the icy water and they got her home before she froze to death. That night, Jo held her little sister until Amy fell asleep. Then, Jo cried in her mother's arms, while Mrs. March kissed Jo's pale, worried face and told her everything would be alright. ■

Jo goes skating with Laurie on the icy river. Amy follows them because she still wants Jo to forgive her. Amy goes on the part of the river where the ice is thin and it breaks under her. Laurie saves her and that night Jo cries in her mother's arms because she almost lost her little sister.

> **Think**
> Have you ever argued with someone and then felt sorry about it afterwards?

[1] skating

After-reading Activities • Chapter 2

Reading B1 Preliminary

1 Choose the best answer, A, B, C or D to complete the text about Chapter 2.

Jo became friends with Laurie and they discovered that they <u>both</u> loved books. She (**1**) _____ met Mr. Laurence and he said Jo was (**2**) _____ her grandfather. Soon they became good neighbors and the girls often visited Laurie's house. At first, Beth was (**3**) _____ shy to go but then Mr. Laurence (**4**) _____ her to play the piano his granddaughter used to play. Beth was (**5**) _____ excited that she forgot to be shy and went every day to play for the old man. She made him a (**6**) _____ of slippers and he gave her a piano.

	A together	**B** every	**C** all	**D** both
1	**A** also	**B** too	**C** as well	**D** besides
2	**A** as	**B** like	**C** same	**D** similar
3	**A** so	**B** quite	**C** too	**D** such
4	**A** said	**B** let	**C** made	**D** asked
5	**A** very	**B** such	**C** so	**D** much
6	**A** couple	**B** pair	**C** lot	**D** piece

Speaking and Writing

21st Century Skills

2 In Chapter 2, the girls do different things in their free time. Answer the questions and write your answers.

1 Beth plays the piano for Mr. Laurence. Can you play a musical instrument or would you like to learn to play one?
2 Amy loves drawing. Do you like drawing or painting in your free time? Why? / Why not?
3 Jo loves reading. How important do you think it is to read? Why?
4 What kind of books do you prefer reading? Why?
5 Meg likes walking in the garden. How much of your free time do you spend outside?
6 How important do you think it is to do some kind of sport? Why?

Grammar

3 Choose the best answer.

Mrs. March let Jo *go* / *to go* and visit Laurie.
1 Laurie came to see the girls instead of *stay* / *staying* at home on his own.
2 Laurie's grandpa didn't want him *to bother* / *bother* strangers.
3 Laurie ought *go* / *to go* out more and talk to people.
4 Jo needn't *to be* / *be* afraid of Mr. Laurence because he's a kind man.
5 Jo couldn't wait *to tell* / *tell* her sisters about Mr. Laurence and his house.
6 Mr. Laurence decided *giving* / *to give* Beth a piano.

Before-reading Activity

Listening

4 Listen to the start of Chapter 3 and decide if these sentences are true (T) or false (F).

	T	F
It was summer now.	☐	☑
1 Meg's friend was coming to stay for two weeks.	☐	☐
2 Mrs. March had bought her daughter fashionable gloves.	☐	☐
3 The Moffat family had a lot of money.	☐	☐
4 The Moffat family never had parties.	☐	☐
5 Meg got flowers from Laurie.	☐	☐
6 Meg wrote a note to her mother.	☐	☐

Chapter 3

Lazy Days

▶ 5 It was spring, and Meg was excited about staying with her friend, Annie Moffat, for two weeks. Mrs. March had bought her daughter new gloves and a green umbrella for the occasion.

"I'm so lucky to have all these new things," said Meg, "even if they aren't the latest fashion."

When it was time to go, Mrs. March kissed her eldest daughter goodbye. She hoped Meg wouldn't come back with her head full of silly ideas. The Moffats were, after all, very rich and fashionable.

The Moffat's house was indeed beautiful and, at first, Meg felt a bit nervous. However, the people were kind, and she soon began to enjoy the lazy days full of parties and fun. It was very different from her usual simple life at home. The more she saw Annie Moffat's pretty things, the more she wanted them.

One evening, the girls were getting ready for a party, when some flowers arrived for Meg. They were from Laurie.

Meg goes to stay for two weeks at the Moffat's house. They're rich and have lots of parties, which is totally different from Meg's usual simple life.

Little Women

"Who are the flowers from, Meg?" asked the girls excitedly.

"Laurie, and there's a note from Mother, too," said Meg.

The others looked at each other and laughed. They obviously thought Laurie was much more than just a friend to Meg. Everybody at the party wanted to know who the "fresh girl with the beautiful eyes" was. Meg was a big success with her simple ways and appearance. Later, she went into the garden for some air. The Moffat girls were there and she heard one say:

"Mrs. March has planned well, hasn't she? Laurie will make a good husband for Meg and the family will solve their money problems too."

Meg's face turned red. She was both angry and ashamed. She went back into the house before they noticed her. She wanted to cry but did her best to appear happy until the evening ended.

The following Thursday, the Moffats had another party. This time, they invited Laurie. Meg had tried to explain that he was just a friend, but the girls didn't believe her. They gave her a tight dress to wear and did her

Meg gets flowers from Laurie and the others think he's more than just a friend. Meg feels ashamed when she hears them saying that Laurie will be a good husband and solve her family's money problems. The Moffats invite Laurie to the next party.

Louisa May Alcott

hair and make-up. When they had finished, there was nothing of the old, simple Meg left.

"You're a little beauty," they said. Meg believed she was like a real lady until Laurie saw her.

"What have you done?" asked Laurie. "You're like a painted doll!"

At first, Meg was angry, then she realized he was right.

"Please, don't tell them at home, Laurie. Mother would be so disappointed in me."

"Don't worry, I won't say a word," said Laurie. "Come on! Let's get some lemonade!"

"Yes, let's!" said Meg, happy to have her old friend again. When Saturday came, Meg was ready to go back home to her simple, happy family life.

That evening, Meg told her mother about the party, and what she had heard the Moffats say.

"Meg, it's normal to like nice things," said her mother. "Just remember, there are more important things in life, like love and respect. And forget what they said about Laurie. Of course, I have plans for my daughters. I want you all to have a happy life, either married or single.

The Moffats make Meg dress differently and do her hair and make-up. Laurie tells her she's like a painted doll and she realizes he's right. Meg is happy to go home to her family. Her mother says that love and respect are more important than nice things and that all she wants is for her daughters to have a happy life.

Little Women

That's my plan." With these words, she kissed her daughter goodnight, and Meg felt safe and loved.

The girls loved games, and they had a secret club, called the "Pickwick Club", for a year. Now that Laurie had become a good friend, he, too, became part of the club. On his first evening as a member, Laurie had a surprise for them.

"To thank you all, I've made a private post office in the garden shed[1]. It used to be full of stuff[2] for the garden and old chairs, but now it's empty and clean."

"Wow! What a great idea!" said the girls.

"I know!" said Laurie, laughing. "We can leave letters, books and any other stuff to send each other. Here are the keys. One for the Marches and one for the Laurences."

The post office soon became an important part of their daily lives. Lots of different stuff passed between the two houses; long letters, poetry and music. Even old Mr. Laurence liked it and sent funny notes, while his gardener sent a love letter to Hannah. They all laughed at this, not realizing how many love letters the little post office would hold in the future.

The girls love playing games and Laurie becomes part of their secret club. He makes a private post office in the garden shed where they can leave messages, books or other things for each other.

---

[1] **shed** small simple building, made of wood
[2] **stuff** things

Louisa May Alcott

Summer came, and Jo and Meg were glad that they didn't have to work for the next three months.

"I'm going to get up late every morning and do nothing all day," said Meg.

"I'm going to read and have fun with Laurie," said Jo.

"Let's not do any lessons, Beth, and play all the time," said Amy.

"Well, I will, if Marmee doesn't mind," said Beth. "There are lots of new songs I want to learn."

Mrs. March was in a corner of the room listening to her girls. "You can do what you want for a week and see how you like it," she said. "But I think you'll find 'all play and no work' as bad as 'all work and no play'."

"Never!" said the girls.

"We'll see," said their mother quietly.

Of course, Mrs. March was right. After a few days, things started to go wrong. Jo had a headache because she had read too much; Beth's pet bird died because she forgot to feed it; Amy got bored drawing on her own, and Meg slept so late that she missed breakfast and had to eat on her own which she didn't like at all.

Summer arrives and the girls can't wait to relax and do nothing. Mrs. March says that all play and no work is as bad as all work and no play and she's right.

Little Women

On Saturday, Mrs. March decided to stay in bed all day, and Hannah went on holiday. When the girls got up, there was no fire in the kitchen and no breakfast.

"Hannah and I have worked hard all week doing your jobs," said their mother. "Now, you can do everything."

Jo decided to take control of the kitchen and make lunch for everyone. What a mistake! She also invited Laurie and Miss Crocker, a poor old lady who lived nearby. Mrs. March went out for lunch. Of course, the food was terrible. Jo hoped her strawberry dessert would save the day, but she had put salt on the strawberries instead of sugar! They were so disgusting that Amy ran from the table. Poor Jo's face went bright red and she wanted to cry. Then, Laurie laughed and soon they were all laughing.

That evening, Mrs March said:

"Do you want another week of lazy days or have you had enough, my dear girls?

"No, give us back our old duties, please," said the girls and Mrs. March laughed happily.

One morning, Beth came in from their post office with a letter for Meg from Mr. Brooke and

Mrs. March decides to leave the girls to do everything on Saturday as they've done nothing all week. Jo cooks but the food is terrible. The girls realize that it's better to do their old duties and their mother is pleased that they've learnt their lesson.

Louisa May Alcott

one of her gloves. He had written the words of a German song she wanted.

"I wonder where the other glove is," said Meg, not thinking for a moment that maybe Mr. Brooke had found both but kept one. Mrs. March looked at her pretty daughter, but said nothing.

The following day, the girls spent the whole day with Laurie and some English friends who had come to visit him. They all enjoyed themselves. They had a picnic, then played some games. Mr. Brooke spent most of the day talking to Meg. He even defended her against the unkind words of the English girl, Kate, who, on hearing that Meg taught children, said:

"In England, it isn't nice for a woman to work."

"Young ladies in America are respected for making money for themselves," said Mr. Brooke.

Meg was grateful to him and smiled. Mr. Brooke seemed very different to her today; not serious and boring as she had once thought, but pleasant and kind. ■

The girls spend the day with Laurie and some English friends. Mr. Brooke is there, too, and he defends Meg when one of the English girls says that it isn't nice for a woman to work. Meg is grateful to him and doesn't think he's serious and boring anymore.

Think
Laurie is American but his friends are English. Do you have any friends or relatives who live abroad or do they all live near you?

Jo's cooking is so disgusting that Amy runs away from the table. Jo's face goes bright red and she wants to cry.

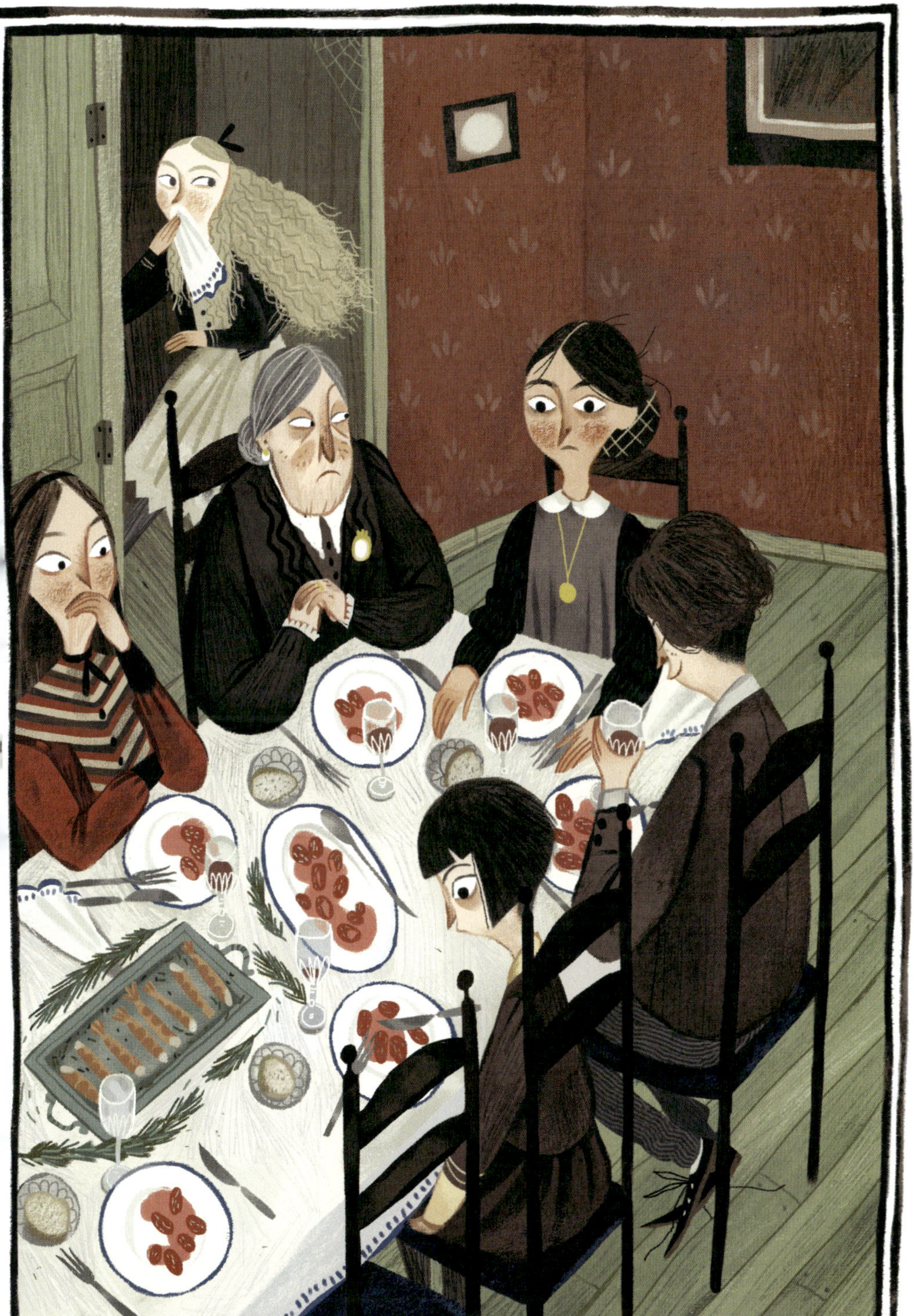

After-reading Activities • Chapter 3

Reading Comprehension

① Answer the questions about Chapter 3.

How did Meg pass the time at the Moffat's?
She went to parties and had fun.

1. Why was Mrs. March worried about Meg?
2. Why did the Moffats invite Laurie to the second party?
3. Why was Laurie surprised when he saw Meg at the party?
4. What did Laurie make in his garden for them to use?
5. Why did nobody like Jo's dessert?
6. What did Mr. Brooke keep that belonged to Meg?

Writing B1 Preliminary

② Read this letter from Annie Moffat and the notes that Meg has made. Imagine you're Meg and use your notes to answer Annie's letter.

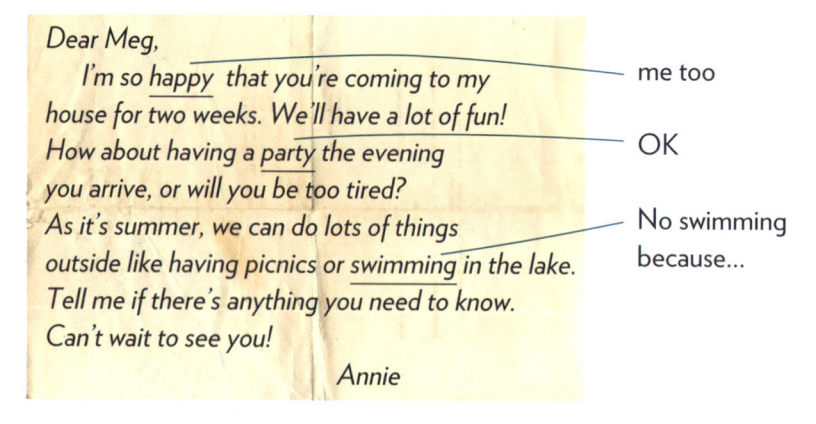

Dear Meg,
   I'm so happy that you're coming to my house for two weeks. We'll have a lot of fun! How about having a party the evening you arrive, or will you be too tired? As it's summer, we can do lots of things outside like having picnics or swimming in the lake. Tell me if there's anything you need to know. Can't wait to see you!
            Annie

— me too
— OK
— No swimming because…

Write about 100 words.

Grammar

3 Complete the sentences with a question tag.

The Moffat family have got a beautiful house, <u>haven't they</u> ?

1 Mrs. March will be glad when Meg comes home again, _____ ?
2 Laurie wasn't pleased when he saw Meg at the party, _____ ?
3 The post office became important to them all, _____ ?
4 Jo had never cooked before, _____ ?
5 Mrs. March knows her daughters well, _____ ?
6 Mr. Brooke would love to talk to Meg all day, _____ ?

Before-reading Activity

Speaking

21st Century Skills

4 Look at this picture from Chapter 4 and discuss these questions with a partner.

1 Who can you see in the picture and where are they standing?
2 Why do you think Jo has cut her hair?
3 What's Jo wearing?
4 What's Amy holding in her left hand?
5 What can you tell by looking at Amy's face?
6 How do you think Beth feels?

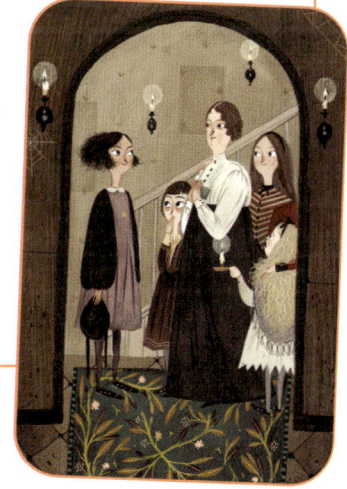

Chapter 4

Busy Bees

▶ 7 One September afternoon, Laurie saw the girls walking up the hill behind their house. They were all wearing big hats. He was bored so he decided to follow them. When he got to the top, the girls were already busy. Amy was drawing, Beth was picking flowers, and Meg and Jo were knitting socks for the army.

"What's happening here today?" asked Laurie. "And why wasn't I invited?"

"Hey, Laurie!" said Jo. "This is the 'Busy Bee Society'. We didn't tell you about it because we thought you might laugh at us."

"Why should I laugh? At least you're doing something useful, instead of wasting the afternoon arguing with people," said Laurie.

"You haven't argued with poor Mr. Brooke, have you?" asked Meg.

"Yes, with him, and with my grandfather. Everybody wants me to go to college[1]," said Laurie.

"Come and sit down and look at our land of dreams," said Beth kindly.

The girls are all busy doing something. Instead Laurie has argued with Mr. Brooke and his grandfather because they want him to go to college.

---

[1] **college** where you study after high school

Little Women

"How beautiful your land of dreams is," said Laurie, looking at the green fields and hills on the other side of the river.

"I have lots of dreams," said Laurie. "First, I'd like to see the world. Then, I'd like to become a famous musician. However, Grandfather wants me to take over[1] his business but I hate ships. I think I'll have to run away, like my father did."

"I'm sure that if you do well at college, your grandfather will let you do what you want," said Meg. "My dream is to have a lovely house full of pretty things and lots of servants."

"I'd have lots of horses, and I'd write books and become rich and famous," said Jo.

"I'd stay at home with Father and Mother, and help take care of the family," said Beth.

"My biggest dream is to be the best artist in the whole world," said Amy.

They all laughed and ran back down the hill for tea. For the moment, their dreams were just castles in the air.

One October afternoon, Jo put some papers in her pocket and went out. She walked quickly along the road until she came to a tall building

> They all talk about what they'd like to do in the future.

---

[1] **take over** (here) continue

Louisa May Alcott

with a dentist's sign outside. She looked around, then walked up the stairs.

She didn't see Laurie on the other side of the road. He was sure she was going to get a tooth out and decided to wait for her. Jo appeared ten minutes later.

"Are you alright? Why did you go alone?" asked Laurie.

"I didn't want anybody to know," said Jo.

"How many did he take out?"

"Eh?" Then, Jo laughed and said: "Two need to come out, but I must wait a week. Anyway, what were you doing here, Laurie?"

"Just talking to Ned Moffat."

"Humph! I don't like that boy," complained Jo.

"Never mind, Ned; tell me your secret, Jo."

"You won't say anything about it at home, will you, Laurie?"

"Of course not!"

"Well, I've written two stories and the newspaper will let me know if they like them next week."

"Brilliant!" shouted Laurie.

"So that's my secret. Now what's yours?" asked Jo.

"I know where Meg's glove is."

Jo tells Laurie her secret. She's written two stories and has given them to a newspaper to read. They'll tell her next week if they like them. Laurie has a secret, too. He knows where Meg's other glove is.

Little Women

"Where?"

"In Mr. Brooke's pocket!"

"That's terrible!" said Jo.

"No, it's romantic," said Laurie.

"Well, I don't want anybody to take Meg away!"

"You'll feel better about it when somebody comes to take you away."

"No, I won't!" said Jo angrily, and leaving Laurie behind, she ran all the way home.

Two weeks later, Meg saw Jo running around the garden with a newspaper in her hand. Laurie was trying to catch her. Then, they both stopped and laughed together for a long time.

"What will we do with that girl? She'll never learn to behave like a young lady," said Meg.

"I like her the way she is; she's so funny," said Beth.

Then, Jo came in and sat on the sofa with the newspaper in front of her.

"Anything interesting?" asked Meg.

"Just a story, nothing much," answered Jo.

"Please, read it to us," said Amy.

Jo began to read and at the end they asked who had written it.

"Your sister," said Jo.

Laurie thinks it's romantic that Mr. Brooke keeps Meg's glove in his pocket. Instead, Jo is angry because she doesn't want to lose her sister to anyone.

Jo's story is in the newspaper! She reads it to her sisters then tells them that she wrote it.

Louisa May Alcott

The girls are all proud of Jo because of her story and soon they'll be even prouder, but not for something she's written.

The girls were so proud of Jo that they all started talking at the same time. They didn't know that soon, they'd be even prouder of Jo, and it wouldn't be for another of her stories.

A few days later, the girls were sitting and talking to Laurie when their mother came in with a message in her hand. Her face was very white and they realized there was bad news.

"Oh Marmee, is there something wrong with Father?" asked Jo.

Mrs. March has bad news. Their father is ill in hospital and she has to go to him at once. Jo goes out to get some things for the journey. When she comes back she gives her mother twenty-five dollars to help pay for everything.

"I'm afraid so. Your father is very ill and is in hospital. I must go to him at once."

Jo was sent to buy some things while Laurie took a letter to Aunt March, asking her for some money for the train journey. Mr. Brooke offered to travel with Mrs. March and she was very grateful. The other girls helped their mother pack. Much later, everything was ready, but Jo hadn't come back yet. Then, the living room door opened and Jo came in. She came over to her mother and gave her twenty-five dollars.

"That's to help bring Father home," said Jo.

"But where did you get the money, Jo?" asked Mrs. March.

Jo has taken off her hat to show them her very short hair. She sold her hair so she could give her mother money for the journey.

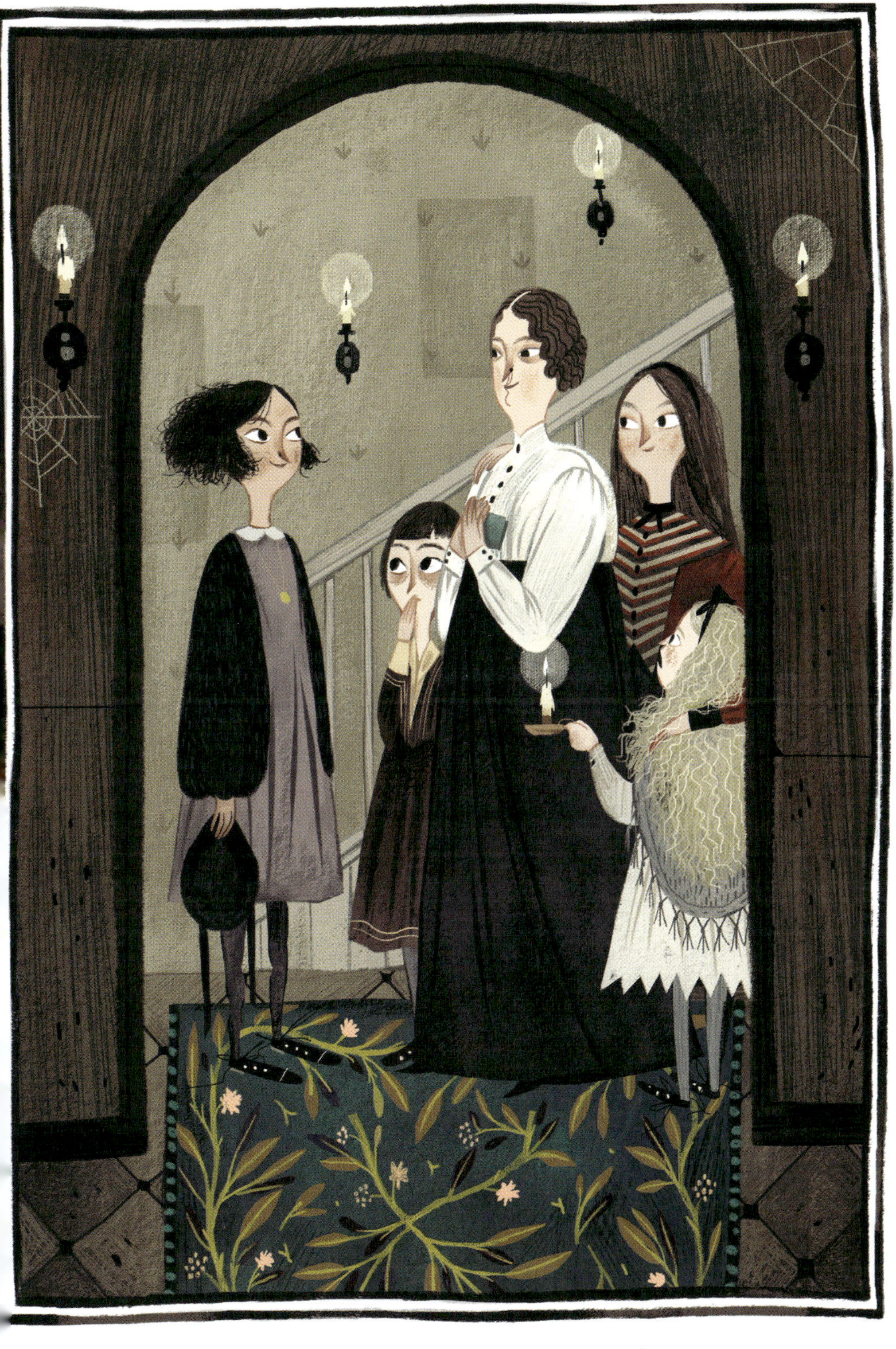

Louisa May Alcott

Jo got the money by selling her beautiful hair. Jo laughs and says she was getting too proud of her hair when she sees her mother crying, but that night in bed, Jo cries herself to sleep.

Jo said nothing. Instead, she took off her hat to show a head of very short hair.

"Oh, my sweet child, you've sold your beautiful hair!" said Mrs. March.

She put her arms around her daughter and held her close, tears running down her face.

"Don't worry, Marmee. Anyway, I was getting too proud of my long hair," said Jo, trying to laugh.

However, much later that night, Jo cried herself to sleep in the dark.

Early next morning, the girls, Hannah, Laurie and Mr. Laurence were all there to say goodbye to Mrs. March and Mr. Brooke as they started their long journey to Washington. When they had gone, Hannah made coffee for the girls.

Everyone is there to say goodbye to Mrs. March and Mr. Brooke when they leave for Washington. Hannah says they must hope and keep busy.

"Hope and keep busy; that's what we must do," said Jo. "I'll go to Aunt March's, as usual, and you'll teach the horrible King children, Meg."

"And I'll stay at home with Beth and help her look after the house," said Amy.

When Meg and Jo left to go to work, Beth remembered that her mother always stood at the window to watch them go.

"Look Jo," said Meg, "Little Beth is being mother to us."

Little Women

"She's such a sweet thing, isn't she?" said Jo.

Mr. Brooke sent them news every day. Their father was still seriously ill, but already seemed a little better now that Mrs. March was there. Each of the girls wrote to their mother in their own way.

Meg chose pretty paper and said how kind Mr. Brooke was to stay in Washington. Jo talked about the time spent with Laurie. Beth sent her mother some flowers she had grown herself. Amy tried to use big words in her letter but ended up making lots of mistakes. However, they all finished their letters in the same way, with lots of love and kisses.

Hannah's letters talked about how good the girls were, and how they all helped her and each other. Even Mr. Laurence wrote. He told Mrs. March to make good use of Brooke and offered her money if needed.

The girls tried their best to carry on their lives as normally as possible, even though they missed their mother terribly. They could never imagine that more trouble was just around the corner and that they would need to be stronger than ever.

Everyone writes in their own special way to Mrs. March while she's in Washington. They all try to carry on their normal lives. They don't know that more trouble is on the way.

Think
What terrible thing do you think is going to happen to the family next?

After-reading Activities • Chapter 4

Reading Comprehension

1 **The following sentences describe what happened in Chapter 4. Put them in the correct order (1 to 7).**

- **A** ☐ Mr. Brooke goes to Washington with Mrs. March.
- **B** [7] Laurie follows the girls one afternoon.
- **C** ☐ The girls write to their mother.
- **D** ☐ Jo sells her hair for twenty-five dollars.
- **E** ☐ Jo reads her story in the newspaper to her sisters.
- **F** ☐ Hannah makes coffee for the girls.
- **G** ☐ Laurie tells Jo where Meg's glove is.

Speaking and Writing

21st Century Skills

2 A **Meg and Jo both work to help their family. In USA, many students under the age of 18 have part-time jobs. Match a job in the box with each picture.**

dishwasher   supermarket shelf stacker   lifeguard
leaflet distributor   busser   babysitter

1 _____   2 _____   3 _____

4 _____   5 _____   6 _____

2 B **Discuss with your partner which job you'd like to do and why.**

Grammar

3 Change the sentence from direct to indirect speech.

"I've argued with everybody today," said Laurie.
Laurie said he had argued with everybody that day.
1 "I have lots of dreams," said Laurie.
2 "My biggest dream is to be the best artist in the whole world," said Amy.
3 "I don't like Ned Moffat," said Jo.
4 "I'll go to Aunt March's, as usual" said Jo.
5 "I have to go to your father at once," said Mrs. March.
6 "A newspaper has bought my stories," said Jo.

Before-reading Activity

Listening B1 Preliminary

▶ 8 **4 Listen to part of Chapter 5. Choose the correct answer (A, B, or C) for each question.**

How long did the girls behave well?
A For a week.
B For a month.
C For a day.

1 Who wrote to them with good news?
A Their mother.
B Mr. Brooke.
C Their father.

2 Who continued doing all their duties?
A Jo.
B Meg.
C Beth.

3 Jo didn't go to the Hummels because
A she still had a bad cold.
B she wanted to finish writing.
C she had a headache.

4 Beth was worried about the Hummels because
A the baby wasn't well.
B she hadn't seen them for a week.
C Mrs. Hummel didn't have a job.

5 How long did Beth wait for Amy?
A An hour.
B Half an hour.
C An hour and a half.

Chapter 5

Dark Days

▶ 8 The first week, the girls behaved perfectly. Then, as good news arrived from Mr. Brooke, they started to relax and didn't keep quite as busy.

Jo caught a bad cold because she hadn't worn a hat. She had to stay at home, and was quite happy lying on the sofa all day, writing. Amy got tired of her house duties and went back to her drawing. When Meg came home after teaching, she wrote long letters to her mother or read Mr. Brooke's letters again and again. Beth was the only one who kept doing all her duties and even some of her sisters'.

Ten days after their mother had left, Beth went to Meg and Jo and said:

"Meg, will you go and see the Hummels, please. You know Marmee said not to forget them."

"I'm too tired," said Meg, who was reading one of Mr. Brooke's letters.

"Can't you go, Jo?" asked Beth.

"Sorry, it's still too stormy for me with my cold," said Jo.

The girls start to relax when good news arrives about their father. Only Beth keeps doing all her duties. One day, she asks Meg and then Jo to go and visit the Hummels, the poor family they helped at Christmas, but they both make excuses not to go.

Little Women

"I thought you were better," said Beth.

"I'm well enough, but I need to finish writing this," said Jo.

"Why don't you go yourself, Beth?" asked Meg.

"I've been every day, but the baby is sick, and I don't know how to help."

"I promise I'll go tomorrow, Beth," said Meg, seeing that her sister was worried.

"I've got a headache and I'm tired. Can't one of you go?" asked Beth again.

"I'm sure Amy will go with you, dear," said Meg. "She'll be home soon."

Beth sat and waited for an hour. Amy didn't come. Nobody noticed as she put on her coat, took some food, and went out in the cold night to visit the Hummels.

It was very late when Beth came home. Nobody saw her go upstairs to her mother's room.

Half an hour later, Jo found her with a bottle of medicine in her hand.

"What's the matter, Beth?" asked Jo.

Beth put up her hand as if to stop Jo, and said: "You've had scarlet fever[1], haven't you?"

> Beth has been to the Hummels every day but she's worried because the baby is sick. In the end, Beth goes herself even if she has a headache and is tired. She comes home late and Jo finds her with a bottle of medicine in her hand. Beth wants to know if Jo has had scarlet fever.

[1] **scarlet fever** a serious illness

Louisa May Alcott

"Yes, years ago, when Meg had it. Why?"

"Oh, Jo, the baby's dead!"

"What baby, Beth?"

"The Hummel baby; he died in my arms."

"Oh my poor Beth!" said Jo. "But where was the mother?"

"Mrs. Hummel had gone to get the doctor, but the baby died before she came back. When the doctor arrived, he said that the baby had died of scarlet fever and that another two of the children had it. Then, the doctor looked at me. He told me to go home immediately and to take medicine before I got it too."

"Oh, Beth, if anything happens to you, I'll never forgive myself," said Jo.

"My head and my throat hurt and I've got a temperature, but I've taken the medicine so I should be fine," said Beth trying to be brave for her sister.

Jo called Hannah and she took control of the situation. She sent Meg to get the doctor, and told Amy that she would have to go and stay with Aunt March because she hadn't had scarlet fever. Of course, Amy wasn't happy with this arrangement.

The Hummel baby died in Beth's arms. He had scarlet fever. Now Beth probably has it. Meg and Jo have already had it but Amy has to go and stay with their Aunt March because she has never had this illness.

Little Women

Luckily, Laurie was there and promised to come and take her out every day.

"Can I come back as soon as Beth is better?" asked Amy.

"Of course!" said Laurie. "And remember, I'll come every day and tell you how she is."

So, Amy went to stay with Aunt March while her sisters looked after Beth.

The girls thought about telling their mother, but Hannah told them to wait.

"Your mother has enough problems with your father. I'm sure Beth won't be sick for long," she said to Meg and Jo.

Dr. Bangs came and said Beth had scarlet fever, but told her sisters that it didn't seem too serious. Then he went and spoke quietly to Hannah. She turned away so that the girls wouldn't see her worried face.

Meg looked after the house while Jo was a patient and gentle nurse. Beth slept most of the time, and when she was awake, she didn't recognize them anymore.

The days were dark and the girls' hearts were heavy as they felt the shadow of death over their

The doctor says Beth has scarlet fever. He doesn't let the girls see how worried he is. Jo stays by Beth's side while Meg looks after the house. Hannah tells them not to say anything to their mother yet as she already has enough worries.

Louisa May Alcott

One morning, the doctor tells Hannah that Mrs. March should come home for Beth. Luckily Laurie and his grandpa sent Mrs. March a message a few days before, so she'll arrive the next morning. Jo is so happy that she kisses Laurie.

once happy home. Everybody missed Beth; Mr. Laurence, his gardener and cook, and all the other neighbors. Shy, little Beth had lots of friends.

One cold December morning, Doctor Bangs came and, as usual, felt Beth's hot little hand.

"Hannah," he said, "if Mrs. March can leave her husband, then she should come now."

Jo ran to send the message to her mother. She came back to find Laurie with a letter from Mr. Brooke. Their father was getting better, but Jo's heart didn't feel any lighter. Laurie held her in his arms as tears ran down her cheeks.

"Jo, listen to me. Your mother is arriving home tomorrow morning. Grandpa and I couldn't wait any longer and we sent her a message a few days ago," said Laurie.

"What? Mother is coming? Oh Laurie!" said Jo, kissing him, "How can I thank you?"

"By giving me another kiss!" said Laurie laughing. But Jo was already in Beth's room, telling the sleeping child that Marmee was on her way home. This good news brought a breath of fresh air into the house and the girls began to hope again.

Doctor Bangs feels how hot Beth's little hand is and tells Hannah that Mrs. March should come home. Beth is very ill

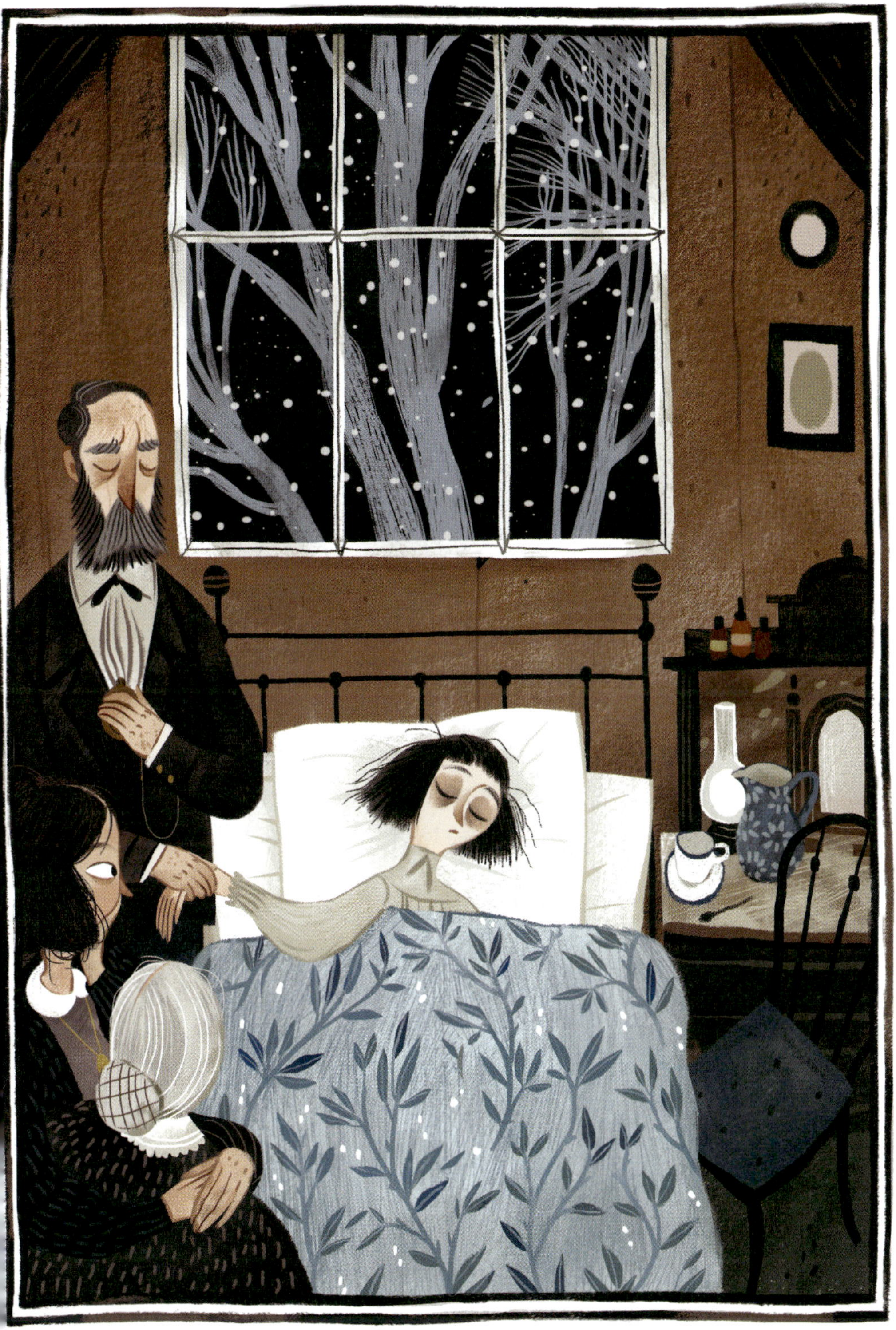

Louisa May Alcott

All that day, Beth slept. The doctor came and said that there would probably be some change, soon. Midnight came and went. The girls thought they saw a shadow cross over Beth's white face.

Laurie left to get Mrs. March at the station. It was two o'clock. Jo looked at Beth. It seemed as if there was still no change for the better. An hour later, the doctor arrived.

"The temperature has gone. She's sleeping and breathing normally," he said kindly.

They all laughed and cried together. Then, Mrs. March arrived and their happiness was complete.

During all this time, Amy had been with Aunt March and she couldn't wait to come home. Aunt March gave her lots of duties to do around the house. She had to feed Polly, the parrot, brush the dog, keep the house clean, and do her lessons! She only had one hour for herself, when Laurie came to take her out. In the evening, she had to read to Aunt March until it was time to go to bed.

She missed Meg and Jo terribly, and worried about Beth all the time. Ester, the house servant, saw that Amy was unhappy, so she let her play with some jewellery and old dresses.

During the night Beth's temperature finally goes down. Then her mother arrives, too, and everyone is happy again.

Amy misses all her sisters and she has to do lots of things for her Aunt March. She only has one hour free when Laurie comes to take her out.

Little Women

One day, when Laurie came to visit, Amy was upstairs playing with her aunt's old dresses. He came into the room as she was walking up and down, wearing a big, long, green dress and a pink hat. Polly, the parrot, was behind her shouting:

"Aren't we fine, ha-ha!"

"Oh, Laurie, how good it is to see you!" said Amy. "That parrot is nothing but trouble. Yesterday, a spider ran under the sofa, and Polly shouted: 'Come out and walk with me, my dear!' That woke Aunt March up, and I had to read to her for the rest of the afternoon! But tell me, Laurie, how is Beth? I miss her so much. I'm so lonely here."

"I'm afraid she's still quite ill," said Laurie, "but don't worry, Amy. Beth is stronger than she seems. I'm sure she'll get better soon."

"Oh, I hope you're right, Laurie," said Amy.

"I'm always right," said Laurie laughing. He wasn't so sure, but he had promised to keep Amy happy, and that's what he would do until she could go back home.

Amy tells Laurie that she feels really lonely at her aunt's and misses Beth. Laurie tries to keep Amy happy until she can go home again.

Think
Who and what would you miss if you had to stay away from home for a long time?

After-reading Activities • Chapter 5

Reading B1 Preliminary

1 Complete the text about Chapter 5 with one word in each space.

The girls behaved perfectly ___for___ the first week, but then Beth was the only one who continued to do (**1**) _____ her duties and not just some of them. The Hummel baby died (**2**) _____ Beth's arms and then Beth got scarlet fever. Amy was sent to stay with Aunt March because she had (**3**) _____ had scarlet fever. Both Meg and Jo had already had this illness (**4**) _____ they could stay at home. Meg helped keep the house clean and Jo looked (**5**) _____ her little sister. After many days, Beth's temperature finally went (**6**) _____ during the night and everyone was happy to see she was getting better.

Grammar

2 Complete the sentences using the correct form of the verb given.

When their father is better, Mrs. March (come) _will come_ home.

1 If Mr. Brooke (not write) _____ every day, the girls would get worried.
2 When Mrs. March (arrive) _____ home, she'll look after Beth.
3 Beth (play) _____ the piano if she didn't feel so ill.
4 Amy (not be able) _____ to come home until Beth is well again.
5 If Amy didn't do her duties well, Aunt March (not let) _____ her go out.

58

Vocabulary

③ Complete the sentences with a word from the box.

| throat | ~~temperature~~ | ill |
| cold | well | tired | headache |

Hannah knew Beth had a ___temperature___ because her forehead was very hot.

1. Beth couldn't eat anything because her _____ hurt.
2. Jo caught a bad _____ because she hadn't worn a hat when it was stormy.
3. After doing all her duties, Amy felt really _____ and went to bed.
4. When the doctor realized how _____ Beth was, he told Hannah to tell Mrs. March.
5. Aunt March got a _____ when Amy made too much noise.
6. Mr. March still wasn't _____ enough to come home.

Before-reading Activity

Speaking and Writing

21st Century Skills

④ A What do you think will happen in the last chapter? Work in pairs and talk about the following people.

Meg   Jo   Mr. Brooke   Laurie

④ B Now use your ideas to write about 100 words about the future of each person. Then, read Chapter 6 and see if you were right.

Chapter 6

Peaceful Weeks

The best medicine for Beth is having her mother home. Mrs. March also goes and sees Amy. The girl shows her a ring her aunt gave her and says she wants to wear it so she remembers not to be selfish. Amy will soon be able to go back home.

▶ 10 The first thing Beth saw when she woke up was her mother's sweet face. It was the best medicine ever! Meg and Jo could finally sleep, knowing that Marmee was there to look after little Beth. Laurie went to tell Amy, and even Aunt March cried a little when she heard the good news. Aunt March gave Amy a ring for all her work. Later that day, Mrs. March came to see Amy. They talked and talked and Amy showed her mother the ring.

"Don't you think you're a little too young for an important ring like that, Amy?" asked Mrs. March.

"It's to remind me not to be selfish," said Amy. "Beth isn't selfish and that's why everybody loves her. I want to be loved as much as Beth, so I'm going to do my best to be like her."

"Then wear your ring, my child," said Mrs. March. "And remember that we all love you and miss you. Soon you'll be able to come home," she said as she kissed Amy goodbye.

Little Women

That evening, Jo told her mother how Mr. Brooke had kept Meg's glove.

"When Laurie saw the glove, Mr. Brooke told him that he liked Meg, but didn't want to say because she was so young and he was so poor." said Jo.

"Do you think Meg likes Mr. Brooke?" asked Mrs. March.

"How should I know?" said Jo. "I know nothing about love and romance. She's still eating and sleeping normally."

"So, do you think Meg isn't interested in John at all?" asked her mother.

"Who?" cried Jo.

"Mr. Brooke," said her mother. "Your father and I started calling him John while we were in the hospital, and he likes it."

"I can imagine!" said Jo angrily. "Now, you'll let him marry Meg just because he was kind to Father. He's been very clever, hasn't he?"

"Jo, don't get angry. Mr. Brooke has indeed been very kind and also very honest. He told us

Jo and her mother talk about Mr. Brooke and Meg. Jo is angry because she thinks the man has been nice to the family so that he can marry Meg. Instead, her mother says Mr. Brooke has always been honest with them and about his love for Meg.

Louisa May Alcott

about his love for Meg, from the start. He says he wants to have a comfortable home before asking her to marry him and I said that Meg is still too young."

Jo wasn't happy at the thought of losing her dear sister to Mr. Brooke, but she promised to say nothing to Meg. Mrs. March promised Jo that Meg would have to wait until she was twenty if she wanted to marry John Brooke, so Jo felt a bit happier. She hated the idea that they were all growing up and that things would change in the family.

Jo spent the next few days with Laurie. Although Jo said nothing, Laurie realized that Mr. Brooke had said or done something about his love for Meg. The boy was a bit annoyed that Mr. Brooke hadn't told him.

Then, Meg began to act in a strange way. She was very quiet and looked worried. Jo was sure Meg was already in love, but her mother told her to just wait and see.

Next day, Jo went to their little post office in the garden and came back with a letter for Meg. Jo sat back down next to her mother and they continued knitting, when suddenly Meg cried

Jo is happier when her mother says that if Meg wants to marry John Brooke she'll have to wait until she's twenty. Jo brings Meg a letter from their little post office and when Meg reads it, she seems upset.

Meg is holding a letter in her hand and she's very upset. Jo and her mother, who are knitting, don't understand what's wrong.

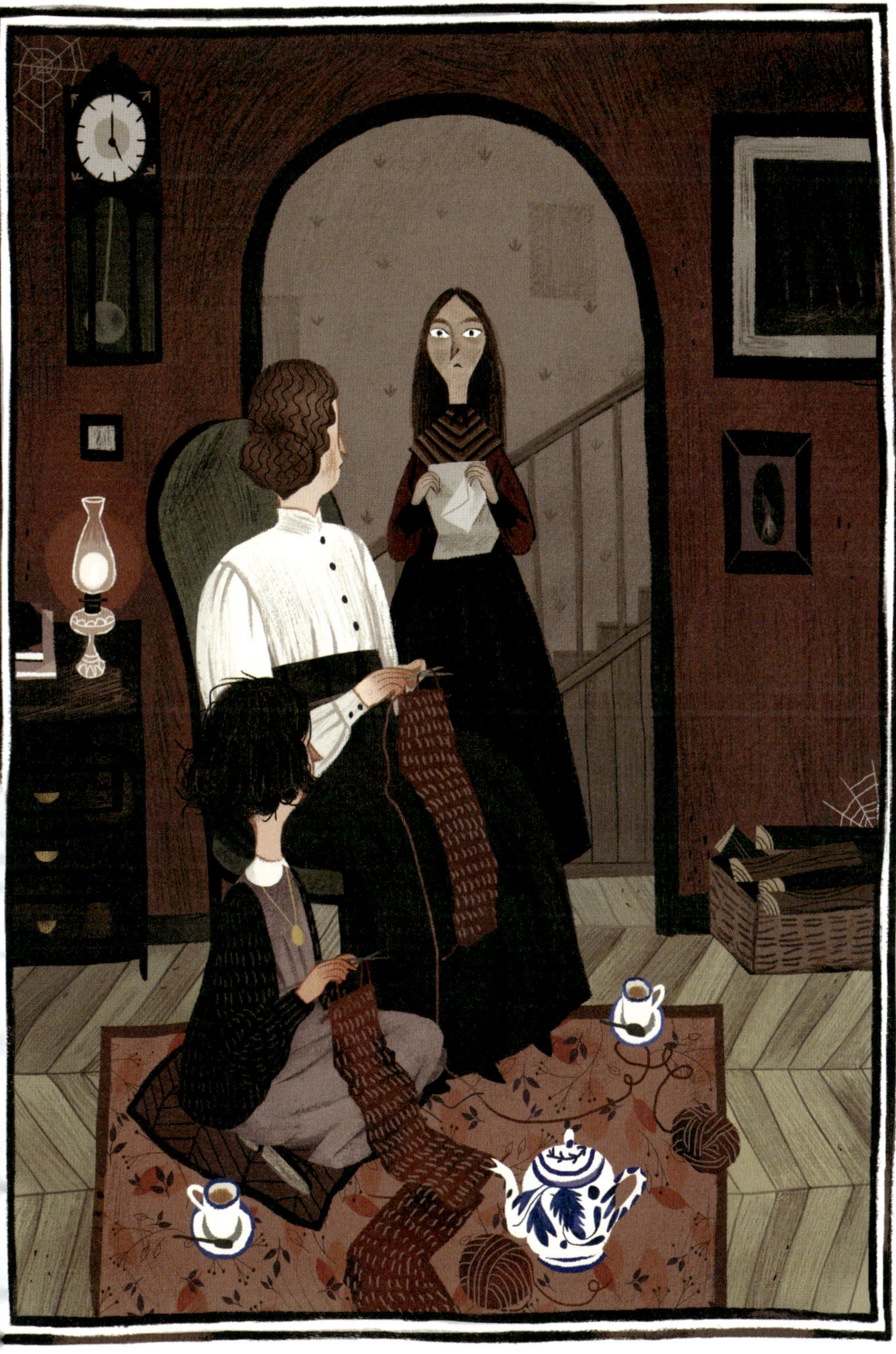

Louisa May Alcott

> **Meg is upset because she realizes that the love letter she got from Mr. Brooke two days before wasn't really written by him. She thinks Jo wrote it.**

"Ooh!". She was holding the letter in her hand and seemed terribly upset.

"It's a letter from Mr. Brooke. He says he didn't send me a love letter two days ago and that it was probably a joke. Oh, Jo, how could you do this to me?" cried Meg.

"What? I didn't write any letter," said Jo.

In the first letter, Mr. Brooke had said he loved her and wanted to marry her. Meg had answered saying that she could only be his friend for now, and that he should speak to her parents.

"This is all Laurie's work," said Jo, as she ran out of the house to get him.

> **Jo realizes it was Laurie who wrote the letters. Laurie says he's sorry and also that Mr. Brooke knows nothing about the letters. Mrs. March tells Meg about Mr. Brooke's true feelings for her.**

"Don't worry, Meg," said Mrs. March. "No damage has been done." She then told Meg about John Brooke's true feelings for her.

"Oh, Mother, I don't want to think about love yet," said Meg. "If John doesn't know anything about these letters, then tell Jo and Laurie to say nothing."

Then Laurie arrived, and after talking to Mrs. March alone, he told Meg he was sorry, and that Mr. Brooke knew nothing of the letters. The joke

Little Women

was soon forgotten, but Meg couldn't forget John Brooke quite as easily.

The following weeks were peaceful. Beth was now able to lie on the sofa where she played with her cats and dolls. She was still weak but no longer in danger. Mr. March was getting stronger and said he might be home by January. Amy was home now too, and looked at her ring every time she felt she might have a selfish thought.

Christmas Day came, and Laurie and Jo had a surprise for Beth. They took her to the window, and there in the garden was a big snowman[1]. There was music playing, and the snowman held a poem for Beth asking her to accept this gift from Laurie and Jo. Beth loved her special snowman and clapped her hands excitedly at the window. Everyone was happy. Beth was well again. Jo had a new book to read. Mr. Laurence had bought Meg her first silk dress, and Amy had received a beautiful picture for her room. Mrs. March looked at her four daughters and felt proud and happy. It had been a hard year but it had made them all stronger. Suddenly, Laurie's head appeared at the door.

Beth is much better and can lie on the sofa and Amy is home too. Their father might be home by January.

On Christmas Day, everyone is happy and Mrs. March feels proud about how they've all managed despite the year being so hard. Then Laurie says there's another present for the March family.

[1] **snowman**

Louisa May Alcott

Laurie disappears and then they see Mr. Brooke with Mr. March - the best Christmas present for everyone. They all kiss each other and Mr. Brooke kisses Meg by mistake, or so he says.

Mr. Brooke comes back to visit Meg a few days later. Meg promises Jo that she'll tell him that they'll just have to be friends because she's too young, but they've been in the living room for ages and Jo isn't sure if eveything has gone as planned.

"Here's another Christmas present for the March family," he said excitedly.

Then he disappeared, and in his place there were two men. They were both tall. The older man was holding onto the younger man's arm. They stood there, tried to say something, but couldn't. Then, they all ran to each other and kissed, and cried, and laughed. Amy was so excited that she fell over the chair and ended up kissing her father's boots. Mr. Brooke kissed Meg by mistake, or so he said, and Jo danced about the room shouting for joy[1]. Mrs. March kissed her husband, then pointed to the sofa where Beth lay quietly. Mr. March went over to her and held her in his arms. It was the best Christmas ever.

A few days later, Mr. Brooke came back to visit Meg. Jo had spoken to her sister that morning and Meg had said that she had already written her speech for Mr. Brooke.

"Don't worry, Jo, you aren't going to lose me yet," said Meg. "I'm going to tell him that I'm too young, so we'll just have to stay friends."

"Well done! That's my Meg!" Jo said happily.

Mr. Brooke appears with Mr. March - a wonderful Christmas present for all the family!

[1] **joy** happiness

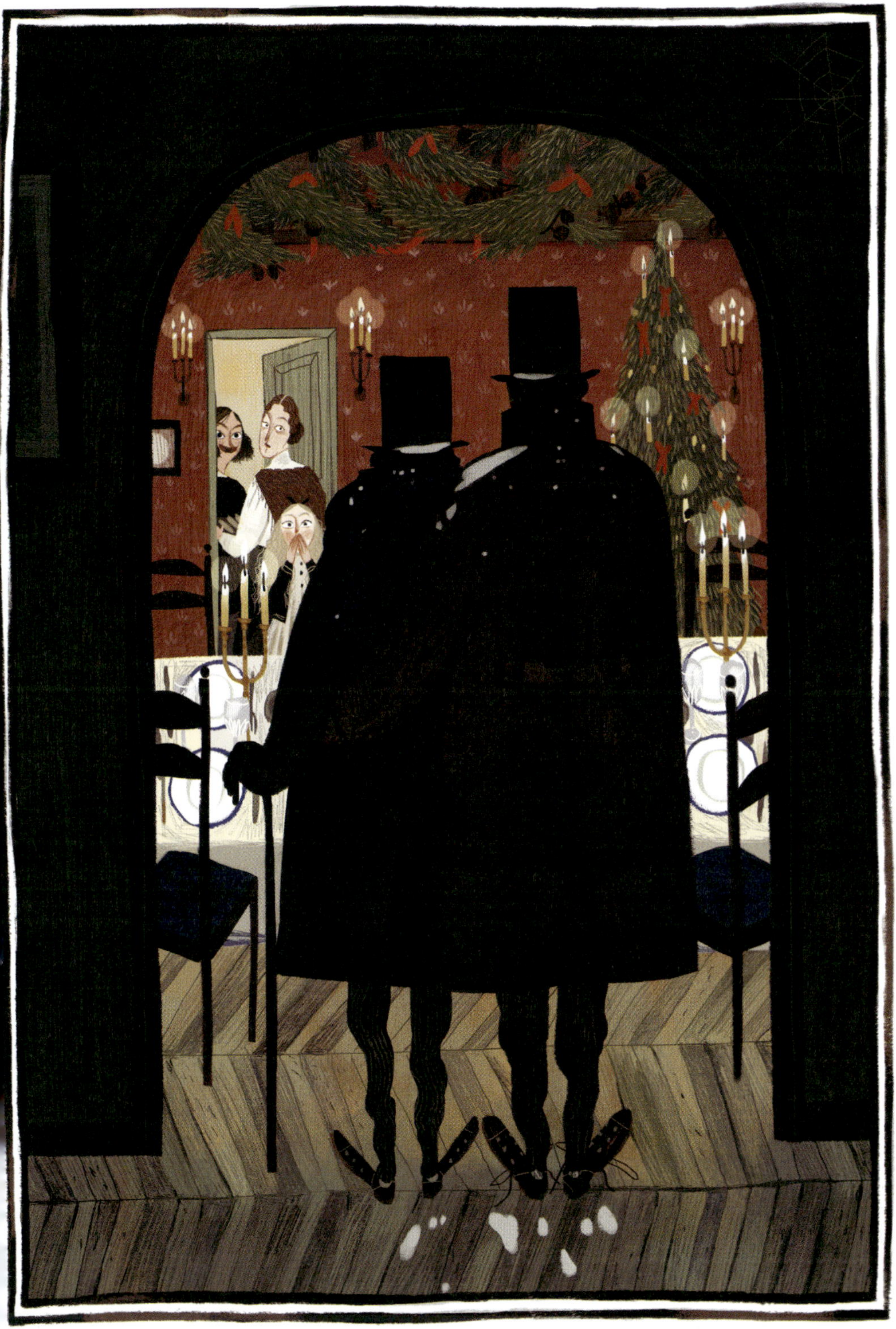

Louisa May Alcott

Jo gets a shock when she sees Meg sitting on Mr. Brooke's knee. Then Mr. and Mrs. March explain the situation to the whole family and even Jo is happy for her sister and this first romance in the family.

But now, Jo wasn't sure that her sister's speech had gone as planned. Meg and Mr. Brooke had been in the living room for ages. She went to get Mr. Brooke's umbrella, to have an excuse to enter the room. She stood at the door for a moment listening. She heard nothing, so opened the door, thinking that Meg had sent him away. What a shock she got! Mr. Brooke was sitting on the sofa with Meg on his knee. He was holding her hand. Jo turned and ran upstairs without saying a word. Mr. and Mrs. March went to speak to the young couple about their plans. Then, Marmee explained the situation to the whole family. They were all happy for Meg now, even Jo! That evening they all ate together. The room was bright with the first romance of the family, and who knows how many others there would be in the future. But that's another story!

>
Jo gets a shock when she opens the door and sees Meg sitting on Mr. Brooke's knee and the two of them holding hands

Think
Which March girl do you think will be the next one to fall in love?

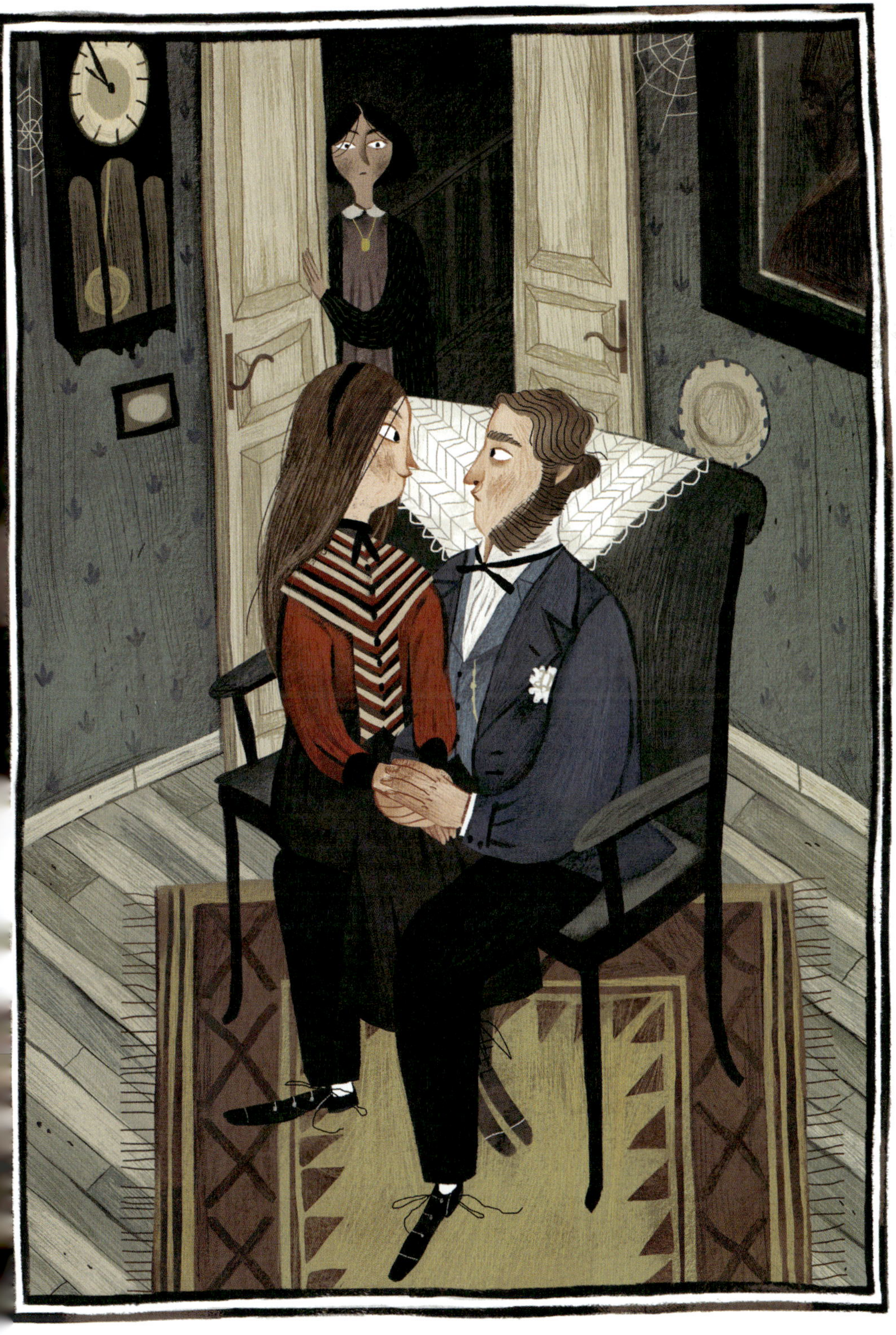

After-reading Activities • Chapter 6

Reading B1 Preliminary

1 Choose the best answer, A, B, C or D to complete the text about Chapter 6.

The girls were all happy that Beth was better and that their mother was ___back___ home. Amy showed her mother the ring she had decided to wear to **(1)** _____ herself not to be selfish. That evening, Jo spoke to her mother and said she didn't think Meg was interested **(2)** _____ John Brooke. Besides, Jo didn't like the idea that they were all **(3)** _____ up fast and that the family was changing. At Christmas, Jo and Laurie **(4)** _____ to do something special for Beth and she loved the surprise in the garden. Then there was another surprise for the **(5)** _____ family. Mr. Brooke appeared with Mr. March on Christmas Day, making it the **(6)** _____ Christmas they had ever had.

	A	B	C	D
	come	to	go	back
1	remember	remind	let	make
2	in	of	about	to
3	standing	getting	waking	growing
4	would	might	wanted	used
5	whole	all	most	one
6	well	good	best	better

Speaking and Writing

21st Century Skills

2 Discuss these questions with a partner and write your answers.

1 Why do you think the book is called *Little Women*?
2 Did you like the story? Why? / Why not?
3 Which character did you like the most? Why?
4 Which part of the story was the most interesting?
5 What can we learn from this story?

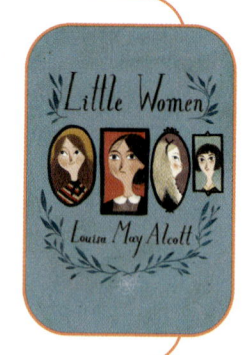

Vocabulary

3 Complete the crossword about *Little Women*.

Across
1. It grows from your head - Jo cut hers for money.
6. A place where you can watch a play. Amy wanted to go there with Meg and Jo.
7. You take this when you are ill. Beth took some when she came back from the Hummels.
8. Something for your nose. Beth gave her mother these at Christmas.
9. A young cat. Beth liked this animal.
10. A meal. Meg missed having this with the others because she slept late.

Down
2. A part of your body. Meg hurt hers at a party.
3. A hobby, Amy was good at this.
4. Red fruit: Jo spoilt these with salt.
5. Something to read. Jo's story was in one of these.

Focus on...

Louisa May Alcott

1832

Louisa May Alcott
American writer, born in Philadelphia, Pennsylvania, on 29th November, 1832.

Family and early life
Like the girls in Little Women, she and her three sisters knew what it was like to be poor, as their father wasn't good with money. Louisa did all she could to help her family, like mending clothes, working as a cleaner, and looking after and teaching children. When the American Civil War broke out, she became a nurse, caring for the soldiers.

Writing and Success

1886

At the age of sixteen, she wrote her first book, *Flower Fables*. Her next book, *Hospital Sketches* (1863) tells the story of her time working in hospital. Then she worked for a children's magazine, but didn't become famous until she wrote *Little Women* (1868). The book was so popular that she wrote *Little Women Part II*, also known as *Good Wives* in 1869. Then followed *Little Men* (1871) and *Jo's Boys* (1886).

1863

Little Women was written in this house.

Later life

With the money she earned from her books, Louisa Alcott was able to give her mother and sisters a better life, and she had the chance to travel the world. She believed all people should be free and fought for a better position for women in society. She never married and despite health problems, she continued to write.

1888

Died
In Boston on 6th March, 1888.

Focus on...

CLIL History

The American Civil War

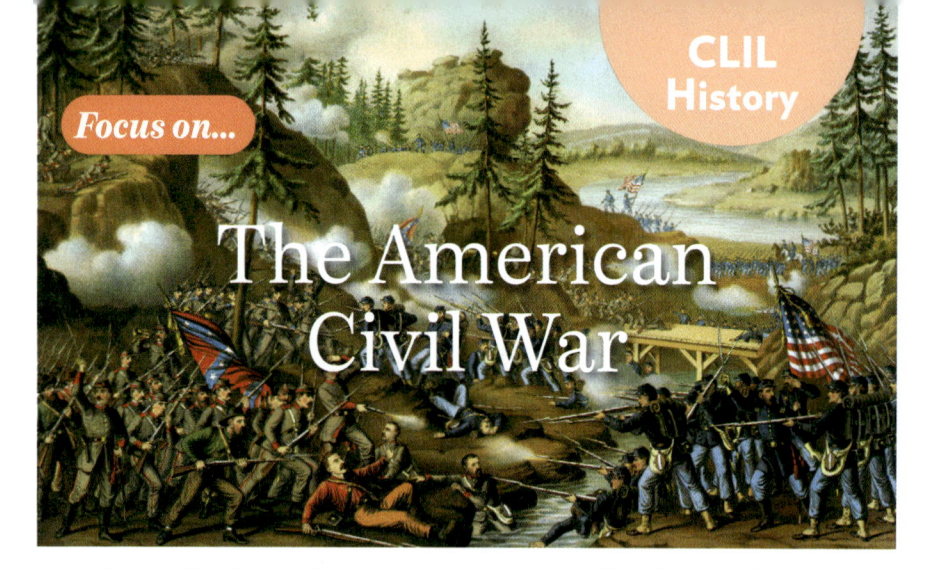

In the middle of the 19th century, many social changes were happening in America and relationships between the North and the South began to suffer. New industries were developing in the North, while in the South they were still only using the land to grow things like tobacco and cotton. Many people from Africa were brought over to America to work in these fields, even if they didn't want to. They were slaves, that is, they were owned by the people they worked for and weren't free to do as they wanted. People in the South became rich by buying and selling slaves and didn't see anything wrong with this kind of business. However, in the North, lots of people wanted the slaves to be free. These people were called Abolitionists and included writers like Louisa Alcott. They believed in the Declaration of Independence of 1776, which said "All men are created equal" and were ashamed to think that slaves were bought and sold in the South. Therefore, these people created the Republican Party and their candidate, Abraham Lincoln, became President. Soon after, South Carolina left the Union of the Northern States. Mississippi followed, then Louisiana, Georgia, Alabama and Florida. In all, eleven Southern states separated from the Union and formed the Confederate States of America (Confederacy) led by Jefferson Davis in 1861. Civil War broke out on 12th April of that same year. The Northern States (the Union) were led by General Grant and, at first, seemed weaker than the Confederate Army. However, in 1865, after beating the Confederate Army at Gettysburg, the Northern soldiers won the war against the Southerners. They signed for peace in 1865 after 4 years of war, in which many people in both the North and the South lost their lives.

Abraham Lincoln (1809-1865)

Abraham Lincoln was the 16th president of the United States from March 1861 to April 1865 and is considered to be one of the greatest U.S. presidents. Lincoln came from a poor family, but studied hard by himself to become a lawyer. He helped create a more modern society with banks and factories, and made travelling easier with canals and more trains. He was always against slavery[1] and, during the Civil War, fought to bring the country together again and let slaves be free forever. He abolished[2] slavery officially with the Thirteenth Amendment to the United States Constitution. He was shot in the head by John Wilkes Booth, an actor and strong Confederate on April 14, 1865, while he was at the theater. Lincoln died early the next morning. Hundreds of thousands of people stood and watched the train that took Lincoln's body from Washington D. C. to Springfield, Illinois where he was buried.

[1] **slavery** the act of owning other people who are forced to work for you
[2] **abolish** to put an end to

Task - Internet search
Find out more about the United States Constitution and describe the following:
- the seven original articles
- the Bill of Rights

Focus on...

Little Women Success over the Years

Little Women was an immediate success when it was first written in 1868. Since then, the story has been used in many forms of entertainment. Let's have a look at some of them.

Little Women at the Cinema

The first two films made about *Little Women* in 1917 and 1918 were silent versions. Then, in 1933, the first 'talking' version was made, starring the famous American actress Katharine Hepburn. She played the part of Jo in the film. The film cost $1 million and took a year to make, with 4,000 people working on it. Like the book, the film was an immediate success and earned more than $100,000 in the first week.

Another film was made in 1949, and the most recent, with Winona Ryder and Susan Sarandon, came out in 1994. In this film, Susan Sarandon was Marmee, while Winona Ryder played the part of Jo, and received an *Academy Award Nomination* as Best Actress.

Little Women at the Opera

There is also an opera of *Little Women*, composed in 1998 by Mark Adamo. It was a huge success. Since then, it has been performed not only in the United States, but in countries all over the world, such as Mexico, Japan, Australia, Canada and Belgium.

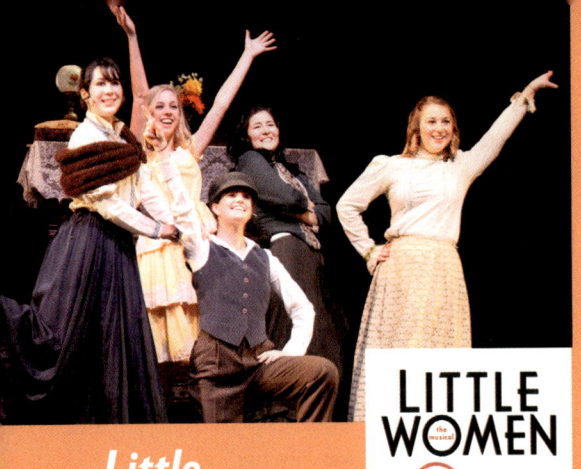

Little Women: The Musical

Jason Howland wrote the music for this musical based on Louisa Alcott's stories about the March family.

It opened on Broadway at the Virginia Theatre on 23rd January, 2005 and was repeated 137 times. It then went on tour and covered 30 cities in the United States. The musical was also performed in Sydney, Australia for a month in 2008.

Little Women on TV

In 1950 and 1958, the BBC showed a six-part series based on *Little Women*. Then, in 1981, a Japanese company, Toei Animation, made an animated television series of *Little Women*. This was followed by another animated version in 1987 by another Japanese company, Nippon Animation. Both series were shown in English on American television.

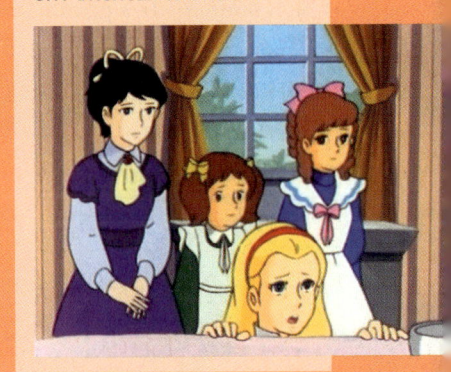

Task

Answer these questions and then check them with the text.

1. Which film version did Katharine Hepburn star in, and which character did she play?
2. Besides the USA, where else did they perform the musical of *Little Women*?
3. Where were the animated versions of *Little Women* shown in English?
4. Name five countries where the opera version of *Little Women* has been performed.

Test Yourself

Choose A, B, or C to complete the sentences about *Little Women*.

At the start of the story, Meg was wearing
- A ☐ a silk dress.   B ☑ an old dress.   C ☐ her party dress.

1 On Christmas night, Mr. Laurence sent the girls nice things
- A ☐ to eat.   B ☐ to wear.   C ☐ to read.

2 Jo went to visit Laurie because he had been ill with
- A ☐ toothache.   B ☐ a bad cold.   C ☐ scarlet fever.

3 The first time they met, Mr. Laurence said Jo was like her
- A ☐ father.   B ☐ grandfather.   C ☐ mother.

4 Meg went to stay with the Moffats for
- A ☐ two weeks.   B ☐ two months.   C ☐ two days.

5 Laurie made a private post office in the
- A ☐ library.   B ☐ garden.   C ☐ study.

6 Laurie's dream was to become
- A ☐ an artist.   B ☐ a teacher.   C ☐ a musician.

7 When Jo sold her hair, she got
- A ☐ twenty-five dollars.   B ☐ thirty dollars.   C ☐ fifty dollars.

8 When Hannah discovered Beth had scarlet fever, she sent Meg to
- A ☐ look for Mr. Laurence.   B ☐ call the doctor.   C ☐ buy some medicine.

9 Polly, the parrot, shouted and woke up Aunt March when it saw
- A ☐ a cat.   B ☐ a dog.   C ☐ a spider.

10 Mr. Brooke's first name was
- A ☐ Robert.   B ☐ John.   C ☐ Ned.

Syllabus

This reader contains the items listed below as well as those included in previous levels of the ELI Readers syllabus.

Verb tenses
Present continuous: future plans
Past simple, past continuous
Present perfect simple, past perfect simple
Future with *going to* and *will*

Verb forms and patterns
Question tags
Verbs plus infinitive
Verbs plus gerund
Phrasal verbs
Conditional sentences: types 1 and 2
Reported speech
Question words
Active / Passive

Modal verbs affirmative, negative and interrogative forms
Could
Should
Might
Ought to
Have to
Need / needn't
Used to

Clauses
Time clauses introduced by *when, while, before, after, as soon as*

Teen ELi Readers

Stage 1
Maureen Simpson, *In Search of a Missing Friend*
Charles Dickens, *Oliver Twist*
Geoffrey Chaucer, *The Canterbury Tales*
Janet Borsbey & Ruth Swan, *The Boat Race Mystery*
Lucy Maud Montgomery, *Anne of Green Gables*
Mark Twain, *A Connecticut Yankee in King Arthur's Court*
Mark Twain, *The Adventures of Huckleberry Finn*
Angela Tomkinson, *Great Friends!*
Edith Nesbit, *The Railway Children*
Eleanor H. Porter, *Pollyanna*
Anna Sewell, *Black Beauty*
Kenneth Grahame, *The Wind in the Willows*

Stage 2
Elizabeth Ferretti, *Dear Diary...*
Angela Tomkinson, *Loving London*
Mark Twain, *The Adventures of Tom Sawyer*
Mary Flagan, *The Egyptian Souvenir*
Maria Luisa Banfi, *A Faraway World*
Frances Hodgson Burnett, *The Secret Garden*
Robert Louis Stevenson, *Treasure Island*
Elizabeth Ferretti, *Adventure at Haydon Point*
William Shakespeare, *The Tempest*
Angela Tomkinson, *Enjoy New York*
Frances Hodgson Burnett, *Little Lord Fauntleroy*
Michael Lacey Freeman, *Egghead*
Michael Lacey Freeman, *Dot to Dot*
Silvana Sardi, *The Boy with the Red Balloon*
Silvana Sardi, *Scotland is Magic!*
Silvana Sardi, *Garpur: My Iceland*
Silvana Sardi, *Follow your Dreams*
Gabriele Rebagliati, *Naoko: My Japan*

Stage 3
Anna Claudia Ramos, *Expedition Brazil*
Charles Dickens, *David Copperfield*
Mary Flagan, *Val's Diary*
Maureen Simpson, *Destination Karminia*
Anonymous, *Robin Hood*
Jack London, *The Call of the Wild*
Louisa May Alcott, *Little Women*
Gordon Gamlin, *Allan: My Vancouver*